Author : Green Rain
https://www.youtube.com/@GreenRain-i8b

Text copyright   2024 by honglee books
All rights reserved.

NO part this book may be reproduced, or stored in a retrieval system, or transmitted in any from or by any means, electronic, mechanical, photocopying, recording, or otherwise, without express written permission of the publisher.

The Heart's *Waymarks*

Life is a series of fleeting moments.
Within them,
we find ourselves constantly questioning
and wandering.

At times,
we crumble under the weight of sorrow,
and at others,
we are dazzled by fleeting beauty.

Yet, when we lose our way,
perhaps a small comfort
or a guiding light
can ease the burden of the journey.

This collection aspires to be
a quiet solace,
a beacon of hope,
and a waymark for those who wander.

Table of Contents

Part 1: Shadows and Solitude 4P
- A Sigh 6P
- Despair 8P
- Emptiness 10P
- Loneliness 12P
- Disarray 14P
- The Sky is Unfeeling 16P

Part 2: Whirlpools of Emotion 18P
- Ignorance 20P
- Regret 22P
- Sleep 24P
- Our Pace is Different 26P
- Falsehood 28P
- Bruise 30P
- To Shed and Heal 32P

Part 3: Traces of Time 34P
- Photograph 36P
- Lost and Gone 38P
- A Painting 40P
- Ember 42P
- Time's Pace 44P
- Find Me Again 46P
- Familiarity 48P
- Traces of Words 50P

Table of Contents

Part 4: Threads of Connection 52P
- Thread 54P
- Seesaw 56P
- Treasure 58P
- At the Table 60P
- Sincerity 62P

Part 5: Growth and Self-Discovery 64P
- Goal 66P
- Thank You 68P
- Change 70P
- The Seed 72P
- Thirst 74P
- A Resolution 76P
- Transformation 78P

Part 6: New Beginnings and Light 80P
- Live Like Water 82P
- The Wolf and the Dog 84P
- The Wind 86P
- Moon 88P
- A Day 90P

Shadows and Solitude

In the quiet embrace of shadows,
we meet our truest selves—
a dance of loneliness and introspection,
where even silence speaks.

- A Sigh
- Despair
- Emptiness
- Loneliness
- Disarray
- The Sky is Unfeeling

A Sigh

A deep sigh escapes into the air.
If only the suffocation inside me
could leave with it.

Even without breathing it in,
this stifling heaviness
slowly builds within.

Worries, fears,
the weariness of life—
they pile up endlessly.

I know the truth.
I need to laugh it out,
cry it out,
and let it all go.

But somehow,
I've forgotten
how to laugh,
how to cry.

Tonight, I borrow the courage of drink,
pretending to laugh,
pretending to cry.
The drink laughs for me.
The drink cries for me.

But tomorrow,
I hope to laugh and cry
with nothing but my own breath.

Despair

I struggle, submerged in a deep ocean.
Even when I fight my way upward,
all I see is an endless horizon.
There's no will left to keep rising.

A rescue ship passes by,
but it does not take me aboard.
It only points me toward the shore,
saving me, then sailing away.

"If you keep going in one direction,
you'll find the land soon,"
whispers hope, softly.

But how long must I keep going?
The unseen weighs heavy,
and fear grows stronger.

Even if it's not the shore,
I wish to find an island—
to stretch my legs,
and finally sleep.

For now, I simply row toward the place
where the sun rises.

Emptiness

Somehow,
I've lost my laughter,
and even sadness
has left without a trace.

Though my eyes are open,
I can't seem to see ahead.

Tomorrow approaches,
but it feels meaningless.
Even out of the water,
I find it hard to breathe.

Everyone's rushing,
leaving me behind.
Where is everyone going
in such a hurry?

If only we could sit together,
share a drink,
and exchange hollow laughter—
that would be enough.

In this quiet stillness,
I wait for someone's voice.

Come find me.
Let's share a meal.
Let's trade stories
and fill this emptiness
with small smiles,
together.

Loneliness

Mayday, mayday,
Is anyone out there?

As everyone laughs and celebrates,
then heads back home,
I cry out loud.

Once, I thought I belonged,
but now, I stand alone.

They say every person
has their other half—
but must I live my life alone?

I long, I yearn,
yet I don't even know
what I'm longing for.

I offer myself to you.
Will you give yourself to me?

I want to be two,
but I always stand alone.

Disarray

So many words in this world
swirl around my ears, adding to the confusion.

Accidents happen,
someone dies,
someone falls ill—
disasters, disease, wars—
so much fills each day.

For all these tragic events,
I offer my heart's sorrow,
but I choose not to be stained.

I sift through and filter,
hoping that only kind, gentle words
remain close to me.

May this world's harsh words fall away,
leaving only the pure and beautiful ones behind.

The Sky is Unfeeling

The sky, from its lofty height,
simply gazes down upon the world.

Its eyes cannot reach every corner,
nor can the divine watch over all,
so it sends people to each other.

Parents, friends, and lovers—
to walk beside us,
to fill the spaces where the heavens cannot.

It seems unfeeling, perhaps,
because it only watches, never acts.

The sky's net is vast and wide;
it seems there's room to escape,
yet nothing slips through in the end.

My actions,
my spoken words,
return to me through those close by.

The sky may be unfeeling,
but humanity is full of feeling.
People may be unfair,
but time is fair to all—
it flows on, carrying each of us
to the same destination.
And so, we simply live together.

Whirlpools of Emotion

A tempest within the heart,
where doubt and desire collide,
and every ripple tells a story of longing.

- Ignorance
- Regret
- Sleep
- Our Pace is Different
- Falsehood
- Bruise
- To Shed and Heal

Ignorance

Why does knowing you
make things harder?

It felt easier,
when I knew less.

The more I understand,
the more familiar you become—
yet, the farther I feel from newness.

When knowing becomes certainty,
it blinds me.
Yet when I admit I don't know,
my eyes open, seeing deeper.

Looking into your eyes, I wish
to discover you slowly,
to know you, carefully.

If only we could meet anew,
growing and learning without end.

Regret

At first, I knew where I was headed,
but somewhere along the way, I lost my path.

Too far to turn back,
too far to sit down and stop—
so forward I go.

Just letting my feet carry me
to wherever they lead,
hoping I'll end up somewhere.

At first, I thought it was meant to be,
but as time went on, it felt more like fate gone wrong.

Too afraid of being alone,
too wary to start anew,
I try once more.

Just letting my heart lead the way,
to wherever it may find its mark,
hoping someday it reaches someone.

Sleep

Quietly,
I push aside my worries and fears,
slipping into the warmth of darkness.

Whispers from ghosts of the past murmur,
"It's too late to change."
Illusions of the future beckon,
"Catch me, and you'll find peace."

I retreat into a thick-walled fortress,
lock the door tight,
and lean against the cold stone.
A breeze slips through the cracks,
carrying fragments of memory.

I rinse away the remnants of emotion:
lingering tear stains,
vanished sighs,
and the burdens I've finally let go.

I gaze upon the silence within me,
softly whispering,
"You've done well today."

For now,
all worries and fears
wait quietly outside the door.

Our Pace is Different

For me, this is all so new.
Isn't it natural to stumble and fall?
It may be different for you,
but can't you understand just a little?

My heart raced ahead—
I pressed the gas,
while you must have hit the brakes.

Then why did you reach out?
Why show interest,
only to tell me to go my own way?

I got ahead of myself, I guess.
Why, though we're together,
does it feel like
you're not here with me?

We're like a coin, you and I—
I thought we were one,
but I'm heads and you're tails.

I thought we were the same,
but maybe we're not.

Could we ever look in the same direction?
Could I ever turn around and meet you there?

You're still where you were,
but my heart has raced far ahead.

Falsehood

How many times a day do I get deceived?
Sometimes I'm the one deceived,
sometimes I'm the one deceiving.

"It's okay now,"
"It doesn't bother me,"
"It'll get better"—

Lies feel more necessary than truth.
I know they're false,
but still,

I think I need them to endure.
It's a lie now,
but maybe someday,
it will grow into truth.

I fool myself,
and I let myself be fooled.

Within the sweetness of falsehood,
I quietly long for truth.
Someday,
I hope this lie will bloom
into something real.

Bruise

It didn't hurt before,
but when it resurfaces,
it aches.

When someone asks,
and it makes me think again,
the pain comes back.

I thought it had healed.
I thought I was fine now.

When the faded colors return,
will I stop remembering?

Will I finally
let it go,
and be able to laugh again?

I apply some ointment,
smile,
talk,
and bury it in the crowd.

But if I bury it like this,
will I truly forget?

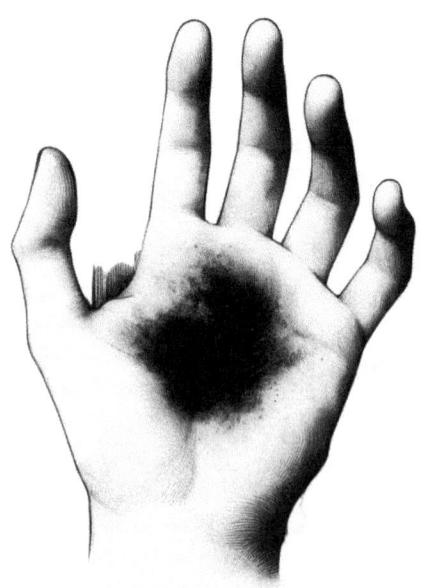

To Shed and Heal

Before I sleep, I face the mirror,
meet my own eyes, and look closely.

I check if any stains of the day remain,
if deep cuts are etched within,
and gently clean and mend them.

Sweet compromises settle on my skin as stains,
and sharp words fly at me, leaving wounds.

One by one, I wipe away the dirt, tend to the wounds,
then hold myself, tired from the day,
letting the tears fall as I think:

Did I become someone else's stain?
Did the words I spoke leave scars?

So I comfort myself, quietly,
and with a gentle heart, I reflect.

Traces of Time

Footprints left by fleeting moments,
where memories linger,
and the echoes of yesterday
whisper softly.

- **Photograph**
- **Lost and Gone**
- **A Painting**
- **Ember**
- **Time's Pace**
- **Find Me Again**
- **Familiarity**
- **Traces of Words**

Photograph

Too precious
to bury in time,
I find myself taking it out,
again and again.

It's fixed here,
so perfectly still.

The warmth of that day's sunlight,
your familiar laughter,
our hands clasped together.

Why is it only the scene that remains?
If only the smells,
the emotions of that moment
were captured too,
how much better it would be.

Unable to return,
all I feel is regret.

I should have kept more,
left more behind.
All that lingers now
is my longing.

Now, the moments frozen in this photo
breathe alone,
as if alive.

Perhaps,
I wish I could be buried
in this photograph of memory,
with you.

Lost and Gone

Where did I leave it?
I can't seem to remember.

My heart, bruised and wounded,
was held so tightly in my arms.

Did it grow legs and run away?
Did it sprout wings and fly?

I never meant to give it away,
afraid it might break again,
so I hid it deep inside.

I cherished it,
fearing scratches and cracks,
but somehow, I must have let it slip.

A heart flows freely,
drifting further the more I try to hold it.

It slipped quietly through my fingers,
and before I knew it,
I had lost it all over again.

A Painting

As I keep painting, again and again,
a picture forms deep in my heart, framed within.

Whenever darkness settles in,
that piercingly beautiful painting appears.

A smile of happiness, the two of us,
from a time when you were always by my side.

Now, only a painting remains of us—
and that's why this picture feels so lonely.

It's my masterpiece, forever unfinished,
left to linger in my own gallery.

With longing, I bring it back to mind,
but brush on ink, knowing it cannot be changed.

Still, when tomorrow comes, it will rise again,
the bruise of memory that will never fade,
the ache of longing painted on my heart.

Ember

A heart you handed me by chance
must have left an ember behind.

It was warm—
the glow I received from you.

It was dazzling—
the ember you gave me.

Your warmth melted my heart,
and your presence
stole my gaze.

The ember grew into a flame,
leaving behind only
a brilliant moment.

Looking back,
my heart, now burned away,
is nothing but ashes.

Yet within the ashes,
a tiny ember still lingers,
flickering faintly.

Time's Pace

Don't leave me behind.
Wait for me.

We can go slowly,
can't we?
I just tripped and fell for a moment.
I just took a wrong turn,
that's all.

I only wanted to live like everyone else.
I only wanted to stay in the middle.

But somehow,
I feel like I've fallen far behind.
When others were running, I ran.
When others were walking, I walked.

I'm not bitter.
Of course,
some of it must have been my fault.

But time, relentless as ever,
keeps demanding
that I pay the price
for all that has passed.

Still, I'll move forward—
slowly,
at my own pace.

Find Me Again

Like the seasons,
returning without fail—
or an unexpected guest
who arrives unannounced,
come back to me like that.

Just as you said,
I won't wait for you.
I won't expect you.

But like the seasons,
when the time is right,
think of me naturally.

Like a guest who comes
only when needed,
just appear and say hello,
with that familiar smile.

Stay for a while or leave again,
it doesn't matter.
Just once more—
find me again.

Familiarity

It felt so natural,
I never even thought about it.
It was just how things were.

I thought words weren't necessary,
thought meeting wasn't needed.

To you, I was that kind of person.
To me, you were the same.

I simply lived, keeping busy.
You were always there,
so I poured my heart into other things.

One day, I looked back
and only an empty space remained.
I didn't even know you had left,
didn't realize you were gone.

You could've said something.
You could've given me a chance.

As I stare at the space you've left behind,
the familiar sight of you
now feels so unfamiliar.

Traces of Words

Words spoken leave a trace,
a mark colored with feeling and thought,
leaving hues upon the world.

Polished, well-chosen words
become signposts for those who follow,

while careless, scattered words
sow confusion and discord.

One by one, each word I lay down—
I hope these colors reach you,
painting your heart with gentle shades.

If only traces of love, gratitude, and care remain,
bright and clear for all to see,
a guiding mark in a chaotic world.

Threads of Connection

In the delicate weave of human bonds,
we find balance,
treasure shared moments,
and speak the quiet truth of the heart.

- Thread
- Seesaw
- Treasure
- At the Table
- Sincerity

Thread

If only I could cut it easily,
sever it with a single stroke.

If only I could cut them all
and fly away into the sky,

or leave for a distant island
across the vast sea.

Even if I were to cast away
my greed, regrets, and hopes,

I find myself tangled
in threads that won't let go—
threads of connection,
threads of fate.

They are easily cut at times,
yet other times,
they refuse to break at all.

They bind me,
and yet,
they give me the strength to endure.

Oh, companion of my life,
this thread may turn me
into a mere puppet,
but it keeps my feet
firmly planted on this earth.

Seesaw

To rise high,
I must first lower myself.

The more I lower myself
to lift someone else up,
the higher I can go.

Only by lowering myself
can others
lift me up.

But if I always try
to stay high,

my partner will leave,
and I'll fall
to the ground below.

When we both lower ourselves
and lift each other up,

we find balance,
meet each other's gaze,
and share a smile.

Treasure

My greed is too great,
so I filled it with everything in sight.

Now, there's no space for more.
Deep inside, it's packed
with dusty trinkets and clutter.

Once, they were precious,
cherished,
radiant.

I must let go,
I must empty it.
Only then can I fill it with something new.

But the more I discard, the more I regret.
The more I empty, the more I want to fill again.
My greed keeps growing,
and I cannot stop this cycle.

Ah, this greedy soul—
it knows nothing of emptiness.

So instead,
I'll fill it only with memories of you,
memories that take no space.

And I'll take them out,
again and again,
to smile each time I see them.

At the Table

You and I,
sitting around the table,
chatting away.

What could be the problem?
It's you and me, after all.

Stories of joy,
stories of anger—
what could possibly
be wrong between us?

I know you,
you know me—
what more
needs to be said?

Nothing, really,
yet we keep adding words,
layer upon layer.

That's who you are,
that's who I am.

In your words,
I see myself.
In my words,
you find yourself.

My time is painted with your colors,
and it makes me happy.
Oh, and tonight—
you're picking up the tab.

Sincerity

I keep wanting
to add more words,
but the more I add,
the more they seem to hide the truth.

That's how lies work.
Layer upon layer,
they must be hidden
to seem sincere.

But sincerity is different.
Whether adorned or bare,
it needs to be expressed fully
to reach the other person.

There's no need to hide it,
so I leave it as it is.

Yet the more I want to show it,
the more I end up adding to it.

And so, in the end,
what is real?
Is it a truth disguised as a lie,
or a lie disguised as the truth?

When words can't convey it all,
silence stands in their place,
speaking for sincerity.

And so, in the end,
it's not words
but the person
that we see.

Growth and Self-Discovery

**Through gratitude and struggle,
we plant seeds of change,
nurturing the thirst for transformation
and finding purpose along the journey.**

- Goal
- Thank You
- Change
- The Seed
- Thirst
- A Resolution
- Transformation

Goal

Hoping to reach it,
I adjust my course, little by little—
and I know I'll get there.

No matter how far away it seems,
as long as I set my direction and follow through,
I'll find myself there someday.

The farther it is, the better.
Even the smallest shift
will lead to a big change.

Eyes wide open,
I just need to keep the focus clear.

Each day lived with purpose
will carry me closer to where you are.

Thank You

I am grateful for the rising sun today,
for the gift of seeing you,
for the chance to hear your voice.

Thank you for simply being in this world,
for the moments we share laughter,
for the comfort of not being alone.

Though life's journey is one we each walk alone,
let us, at times, sit together and share our stories.
The comfort I feel in not being alone—
I hope it reaches you, too.

So please, tell me your worries, your burdens, your pain.
I may not be able to carry them all,
but I'll gladly share them with you.

With hands folded, I pray
for your happiness always.

Change

Little by little,
it piles up.
Bit by bit,
it leaves its mark.
What will it become?

It cannot happen in an instant,
so I earnestly hope
to grow into the image I long for.

To fill myself only
with what is good and precious,

I reflect on who I am
and live each day with care.

Like water becoming clearer,
like light becoming purer,
grow a little clearer.
Grow a little purer.
Grow a little warmer.

My hopes and dreams pave the path,
and on that path,
I simply walk.

The Seed

Everyone carries a seed,
hidden deep within their heart.

A warm and bright mind
feeds it with nourishment,

while a cold and dark mind
supplies it with water.

Too much warmth, too much light,
and it cannot grow.
Too much cold, too much darkness,
and it cannot thrive.

It's easy to smile for yourself,
but hard to smile for others.

It's easy to show anger to others,
but hard to be angry at yourself.

To bloom into a beautiful flower,
a seed needs balance—
just enough nourishment,
just enough water.

And when that seed blooms,
its flower will resemble
the heart that nurtured it.

Thirst

In my dry throat,
a scratch like grains of sand lingers.
I long for a single sip of water.

As the stream flows down, quenching my thirst,
I am reminded—I am alive.

This body's thirst can be eased with water,
but the emptiness in my heart,
what can quench that?

Meaning scatters like grains of sand,
emptiness drifts away on the wind.
Before I knew it, the soil of my heart
had turned into a desert—
cracked, dry, desolate.

If only rain could pour down,
refreshing and cool.
If I could laugh again, cry again,
and find gratitude in each small day,
would it ease the thirst of my soul?

Even a single drop of rain
to touch this parched ground—
if that were to fall,
perhaps the long drought would end,
and perhaps,
I could love people once more.

A Resolution

I told myself not to think of it anymore,
I promised not to let it haunt me,
I swore I wouldn't care.

But why does it keep catching my eye,
why does it echo in my ears,
why does it drift through my mind?

I should just let it flow,
let time bury it deep.

Yet somehow, it's soaked into me,
leaving a lasting trace—
and I can't help but remember.

It's carved so deep within,
a wound that aches,
again and again.

Transformation

Desiring too much,
the flames of greed ignite,
burning oneself to ashes.

Like drifting clouds, free and unbound,
let go, share a little,
and escape the mist of attachment.

Yearning to know too much,
the seeds of doubt sprout,
slowly enveloping oneself.

Like flowing water, calm and gentle,
forget a little, be deceived a little,
and step away from the race of restlessness.

With detachment as my compass
and ease as my companion,
I may awaken from this slumber
to discover a path unlike any before.

As I walk that path,
perhaps, at last,
I will find myself.

New Beginnings and Light

As the wind whispers and
the moon guides,
we flow like water,
embracing each new day
with quiet strength and radiant hope.

- **Live Like Water**
- **The Wolf and the Dog**
- **The Wind**
- **Moon**
- **A Day**

Live Like Water

Knowing where to go,
it flows to the lowest place in the world.

When blocked, it naturally turns,
yet, in time, it will break through.

It can take any shape,
and it can embrace anything.

It never grows angry,
but gently flows
to where it needs to be.

Quenching thirst,
nurturing all life,
it gives without effort,
simply by being.

Whether dirty or clean,
it doesn't mind—
drop by drop,
it gathers to form
the vast ocean.

And then, it returns to the beginning,
seeking a new path,
flowing on once more.

The Wolf and the Dog

As I step outside,
I think of a lone wolf
wandering across the white snowfield,
under the blue moon.

Its footsteps are deep and solitary,
its breath slicing through frozen air.
The chill awakens my senses,
and I find solace in its loneliness,
as if it mirrors my own.

I gaze at the blue moon,
and once again,
I remember the ideals I dreamed of.

Finally, returning home,
I lie down to rest,
and my thoughts turn to a white dog,
basking in the gentle warmth
of the sun,
on green hills by a flowing stream.

Its peace dazzles me,
and I ask myself:

When will my days
be spent solely
with the white dog?

The Wind

Blown here and there,
pushed by the wind.

Following my heart,
I try a little of this,
a little of that.

Carried by the breeze,
my hair dances,
my heart sways.

I'll kick off the ground
that holds me still,
and let myself fly.

No chains to bind me,
no cage to hold me—

Where can't I go?
What can't I do?

And if it doesn't feel right,
I'll just lie back,
look up at the sky,
and let it be.

Moon,

Oh Moon,
do not envy
the brightness of the Sun.

Though it shines alone,
blinding everything around it,
you—

With your soft, quiet glow,
are surrounded by countless friends.

Unlike the Sun,
who scorches the world at noon,
demanding everything conform to its heat,

You light up the night,
changing shape,
yet always mindful,
always kind.

Sometimes, the world doesn't need
the Sun's intense passion,
but rather,
your quiet,
unassuming warmth.

A Day

With weary eyes, I lift my gaze,
force down the food that fills my throat,
and step outside to face the day.

To earn the next meal,
I burn myself away,
and bury today beneath my feet.

I return home once more,
eat once more,
and sleep once more.

When was the last joyful tomorrow?
The last happy day I knew?
It blurs, like memories through a haze.

Joy, loneliness—
all rising like smoke,
fading away into air.

Toward the day without a tomorrow,
silently, I pass through today.

www.ingramcontent.com/pod-product-compliance
Lightning Source LLC
LaVergne TN
LVHW012031060526
838201LV00061B/4562